Weave magic into your life
By
Esme Kent

loveamore

Dream a dream.

Wish on a star.

Keep a song in your heart.

Weave magic into your life.

Weave magic into your life

By
Esme Kent

loveamore

Copyright © 2021 by Loveamore Pty Ltd

All rights reserved. No part of this book may be reproduced in any manner whatsoever without written permission except in the case of brief quotations embodied in critical articles and reviews.

First Printing, 2021

CONTENTS

Forward	viii - ix
Using this book	x
Weaving magic	1 – 96
About the Author	97-98
About the Artist	99
Other titles	102-103
Socials	104

FOREWORD

By Victoria Kent

Mum was always sharing quotes, poems and sayings with my sister and I, we'd pin them to our walls and dream big dreams, think big thoughts. This was long before the rise in popularity of affirmations it was just something Mum did to help us see things differently, to help motivate and inspire us.

Winston Churchill once said, "people remember quotes", this stuck with Esme, having waded through many biographies as an avid reader Esme finds wonder in people's achievements, in people's adventures. It struck Esme throughout all that reading that there were those few outstanding moments, those few words that inspired, beautiful sentiments amongst the sea of words those precious few that spoke to her.

What captivating thought could change the direction of a life, what idea could inspire or motivate an individual, what speeches encouraged armies to keep going, or a person to make a change in their life?

Motivating yourself, motivating people, millions is spent every year on life coaching, psychologists, motivational programs to help inspire, motivate, a call to action for the mind, body and soul.

This book came about out of those insights, they say there is nothing new under the sun, we see things reinvented, TV series and movies are classic. Fashions come and go and come again. Esme has taken inspiration provided to many, motivation given to armies and reshaped, redesigned the words, the sentiments, the ideas in a fresh new way for a new generation, a new era, a new 21st century mind.

Let us therefore brace ourselves to our duties, and so bear ourselves that men will still say: 'This was their **finest hour'**.

Winston Churchill

What will be your finest hour? Is it this moment, a word, a new idea, or perhaps a new perspective.

In finding a new perspective, a different way of sharing a thought, a new outlook, an open mind, an inspired heart. Finding re-invention in ourselves, finding magic, weaving magic into our lives.

USING THIS BOOK

The most obvious way to read the book is just to read it, however below are a couple of suggestions and other ways you can use this book to truly benefit from the wisdom of the thought in each one of the quotes provided.

For example, are you seeking answers? Do you have a situation in your life you want clarity around? Then one way to use this book is to ask yourself a question, ponder it, and then with your eyes closed flick backwards and forwards through the book until you feel like stopping on a page, and stop. What do the words say? Do they help? Is there an answer there for you?

Or, perhaps pick one a day or one a week to read to think about. Write it on a sticky note on your mirror or in your diary and then record your own thoughts and feelings that come to you after reading the quote and as the day or week unfolds.

Laughter shrinks big things into little – it's a recall to sanity

Having known joy, laughter and happiness you can't unknow it.

When something feels right it's usually right – listen to the whispers of your heart.

Mistakes are okay, who said you had to know about life before living it.

Doing one brave thing gives you courage forever.

Testings come to remind us of the bigger spirit self.

Delight in your own specialness, the world wouldn't be complete without you.

Iron runs through a star – Iron run through our blood – We are all recycled stars.

Hope comes each day all shiny and new in a gift wrapped present we have to undo.

Keep trying not every great thing was a big hit right away.

When something feels right it's usually right – listen to the whispers of your heart.

Surprise yourself take it easy, think about what's going well.

Summon your courage, magic your wisdom – those hidden strengths born new every day.

Miracles are everywhere, fancy walking here on planet Earth that's sweeping around the sun 180 million miles across.

Why mistrust the past with it's troubles and mistakes it has given you the heart of a lion.

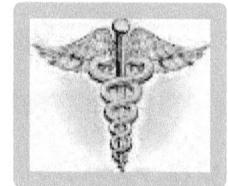

Those thoughts that want the best for you – make friends with these.

"Proverb" Just when the caterpillar thought the world was ending – she turned into a butterfly.

Your life is your story it's a touch of wonder given to everyone.

Each day unknown, tomorrow invisible, living is about walking forward not knowing where we are going – we are all heroes.

Summon your courage, magic your wisdom – those hidden strengths born new every day.

Try not to give up today be a little braver.

Forgiveness helps us transcend, none of us are blameless, but we all, each one of us can forgive and be forgiven.

Hidden talents often don't emerge until they find what they are looking for.

Follow your own heart, why follow someone else.

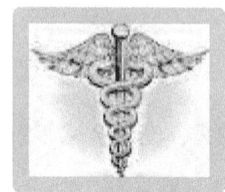

You think you live in the world when in fact the world lives in you – there are over fifty trillion cells in our body, if that isn't a universe, a world of its own, nothing is.

New golden sun invites you to believe – today something wonderful could happen.

I am myself I believe in me. I trust my instincts I know they are true. I grow more like myself every day.

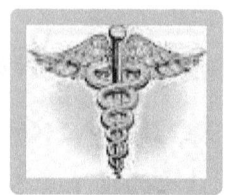

Acknowledge your sense of the mystic, you are not here by chance – it is your destiny to be here. Hold your head high like the timeless mountains, glimpse your immortality in the stars.

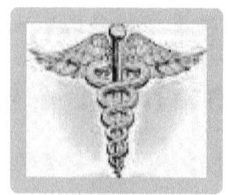

There is not enough darkness in the world to put out the light of one small candle.

The wounded make the best healers – it's the blessing of burden.

What comes from the heart touches the heart – kindness, helping others gives humans their magnificence.

After sad times brave heart smiles to the music and laughter that has long been silent.

Sunrise, sunset, pathways of gold to thank mother Earth.

A sweet hurt

love in a teardrop

on a cheek.

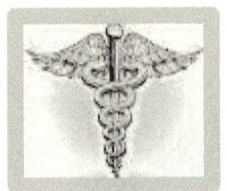

Laughter defends us from the million shocks of living.

How well we learn to fear – but once we lose that fear, hey world watch out.

When you are alive it's quite easy standing up for yourself.

Tough times are not the end of the world, they are part of it.

Controlling ourselves we discover great strength, avoiding controlling others we discover great wisdom.

Knowing I can't change others is knowing others can't change me.

There are no limits within you and within you is where you are.

Life isn't a test so you are not going to fail.

Tough days we take the fall – bruised but not broken.

We have to climb the mountain to learn the climbers lesson.

Trusting yourself is knowing where ever you are the right pathways appear.

Each one of us is that me travelling through Earth with the courage of any explorer.

You are born into your own life to be in charge of it, who knows what you need better than you

May look empty but there's always a rainbow inside a bubble.

Outdoors walking close to Earth, collecting lost pieces of myself.

Only on our knees do we see life through the eyes of a child.

Are we somebody? Or maybe nobody perhaps we are just everybody all brothers and sisters.

With books you are never alone – it's sharing the companionship of someone else's thoughts.

Home is not always where you live, it is where others understand you.

Divinity is saying your life is your great work of art.

Never underestimate anyone – the good news is no-one should ever underestimate you.

Imagination allows you to fly into a flower and touch its soul.

Night time stars crammed with Heaven, warming hearts renewing spirits.

Divinity is saying your life is your great work of art.

Many things are left undone because they have never been attempted.

Keep busy – a moving target is tougher to strike.

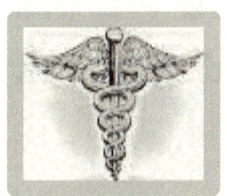

Dear Universe

I owe a lot to you, count me in, I'm your friend.

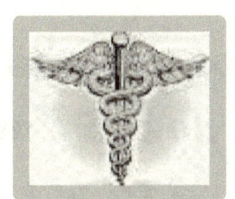

Solitude awakens the stranger within – there we discover what is real and what is pretend.

Feeling sometimes are just feelings, doesn't mean we always have to act on them.

**I believe undiscovered worlds
are out there, better the chances
of nothing.**

**Little children – dreamers of the
biggest dreams.**

It's good to spend some time within yourself – it's always there for you.

Hope like stars fixed on the unseen.

Solitude awakens the stranger within – there we discover what is real and what is pretend.

Intuition has x-ray vision and can see through most problems.

Splash your face, open your heart, stop playing small.

Un-worry about tomorrow you can't deal with what you can't see.

It's giving away your power holding someone else responsible for your happiness.

Why reward and keep close annoying habits you are trying to lose?

Goddess woman, divine feminine within, leader of your destiny, keeper of your soul.

Hands off! Letting someone be themselves is releasing something that never belonged to us anyway.

We don't have to agree fully and give up entirely to ease difficult situations.

Hard times bring pain – pain leaves scars. The wisdom of scars is they make you wiser.

Thinking you are right all the time makes everyone else in the world wrong.

Mind thinking does suppose the heart with feelings always knows.

Believing is leaping into the arms of the universe knowing it will catch you.

Look for the things that speak to different parts of you.

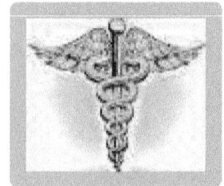

Celebrate yourself, spread your wings, feel the energy the super powers of new adventures. Make a wish.

Love and laughter of angel wings flutter in everyone's heart.

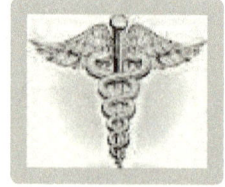

Between today and tomorrow and a handful of stars, expect the best.

Simple is gratitude, like a patch of sun on a gritty road.

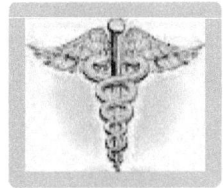

There is always enough of life to spend a perfect afternoon doing nothing.

Clouds floating, painting pictures, where are you going?

If love can persuade you to find tenderness when dealing with others – this is the one true thing.

Sun, moon, stars – me rising brand new every day.

We can do the work of angels because we all have the gifts of heaven.

Without words a smile lifts you above the crowd.

In hard times courage replaces sadness.

Silence gives a new outlook on life – we need silence it touches the soul.

If you don't have someone, find someone.

Heaven's music in the glad wings of butterflies.

Liberate yourself – let your light shine.

Optimism is seeing an imperfect world perfectly.

We are the dream, the power, the gift.

The fine lines of both sweetness and sorrows create a beautiful face.

Think about the people in places that warm the heart, you are at your best when you are truly where you belong.

Just for fun why not dodge those critical remarks sometimes others throw at you – you don't have to catch them.

Open your heart sit back relax let others tell their stories.

Relax, wrinkles are only tense muscles.

Age proof yourself, stay young at heart.

Do you feel the world depends on you, do you think for one moment we are in charge? Can you stop the rain falling or change the direction of the wind?

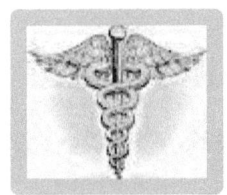

When you seek the best in other's they will show it to you.

We rise to fall, we fall to rise, life is nothing, but endless surprises.

There are strong ways ahead and
many tangled paths to tread –
but I have dreams to me I owe ad
many places still to go.

Life is wonderful and its great,
just being somewhere.

Strike back with individuality if one of us wins, we all do!

Dreams take us away from small crowded places.

Who needs reasons, go with the day, where ever it flows, where ever it goes.

Helping others is a glimpse into your own special goodness.

You are born into your own life to be in charge of it – who knows what you need better than you.

Trusting yourself is knowing where ever you walk the right pathways appear.

Today I am going to wear my coat of gladness.

When we are loved we have to give more because we have more.

Make sure your life has you running through it.

Busy Mother whilst she was building a small home filled with love – a palace was being built for her in heaven.

Spend time with nature and the perfect feelings find you.

It's better to fight shoulder to shoulder than toe to toe.

Being yourself strikes fear into the hearts of those who would conquer you.

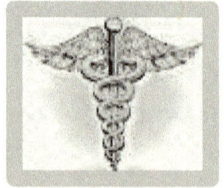

Take yourself lightly and your spirit will fly.

Laughing, crying, singing, weeping – feeling life both sides on.

Out walking natures silence tugs with pleasure at the heart.

To believe in the power that created the sun draws us closer to the stars.

Most days different people refresh our lives.

Could be forgiveness cures many ills.

If everyone gave up, we'd have no brave stories to tell.

In adversity some people need crutches, others find wings.

Last poem in the garden, the mystic light of a human prays.

Night river bathing, washing myself, with handfuls of stars.

Forget the past, try not to worry about the future, each one day is lifetime enough.

Everything about you is unique and different, a one off miracle unfolding ourselves into the world.

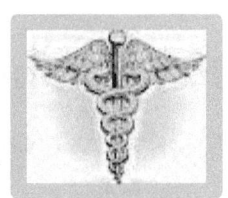

Destiny is knowing there is a place on Earth only you can fill.

Sharing life is rich and precious, life is too good to be kept to ourselves.

There's room for everyone, come lets get together and make the world a better place.

Make big plans, aim high, they will stir you up into doing something.

Each new day, a different light to see myself in watching sunrise and sunset, the greatest show on Earth.

Being yourself takes the heart of a warrior, chin up courage has it's camps.

Let your light shine, see how far it throws it's beam into a troubled world.

Everywhere is here, life is a living adventure wherever you happen to be.

Tough times are not the end of the world, they are a part of it.

You are worth more than the word can't.

Surviving tough times notches courage in the soul.

Take all those impossible out of your heart and start again. I'm possible.

True nobility is not trying to escape life, but prevent life escaping you.

Special dreams are given to you because only you have the power to make them come true.

You are worth more than the word can't.

Surviving tough times notches courage in the soul.

I'm that me travelling through Earth with the courage of any explorer.

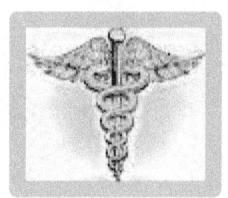

About the Author

Esme Kent

Brave volunteers . . .

Esme has some wonderful stories to tell, from her days as a causality evacuation medic with the Royal Air Force to running boarding schools in outback Australia.

An active community member, volunteering as the first female to go on a live rescue in the wild Irish seas to dedicating years as a crisis telephone counsellor and Justice of the Peace.

Writing articles for local papers as well as writing historical ballads, children's stories and poems

Esme achieved a black belt in Karate when she was 58 years young and she went on to walk the Bibulmum track from end to end when she was 60 and for her 70th birthday became a pilgrim walking the Camino de Santiago trial in Spain.

Esme has delved into many writing genres, even doing a stint teaching creative writing in Esperance, Western Australia.

Esme celebrated her 54th wedding anniversary recently and has two daughters and a grandson.

Art by Kelly Williams

The loveamore logo is original artwork from artist Kelly Williams.

Kelly Williams is best known for her colourful, detailed and realistic artworks. The West Australian artist, who is also a TV news reporter, creates bespoke artworks in a variety of mediums.

Kelly has been commissioned to illustrate children's books, paint custom pet portraits, design business logos, create tattoos and transform memorable moments (captured in a photograph) onto paper or canvas.

From a small Country WA town called Wongan Hills, Kelly has grown up being surrounded by beautiful landscapes, people and animals. Now she attempts to convey such beauty through her art.

Loveamore's Other titles

A collection of poems from the soul for the soul, may words bring to life memories, feelings and emotions that move you, inspire you, ignite you as many moments have inspired this collection. With wonder we walk through the world, with sadness we see it's pain, with joy we experience it's beauty., with hope you will find beauty and inspiration in these words, from my heart to yours with love, peace and blessings.

Bonnie is a beautiful and loveable dog, she loves to say hello to people and she has many adventures meeting many new friends when she is out and about on her walks. Join Bonnie on her adventures meeting various animals showing the amazing wildlife you can see while just out walking in the suburbs of Quinns Rocks, Butler, Jindalee, Yanchep and Two Rocks in the State of Western Australia. The book uses real life photographs of Bonnie the dog meeting different animals, it is a fun story giving clues to each animal so the reader can guess what they are from the picture and verse.

loveamore Instagram

Socials

Follow loveamore for news of upcoming releases.

loveamore Facebook

www.ingramcontent.com/pod-product-compliance
Lightning Source LLC
Chambersburg PA
CBHW022019290426
44109CB00015B/1230